THE FOGGIST

ALSO BY DEAN YOUNG

Design in X
Beloved Infidel
Strike Anywhere
First Course in Turbulence
Skid
Ready-Made Bouquet
elegy on toy piano
embryoyo
Primitive Mentor

THE FOGGIST

A Chapbook

Dean Young

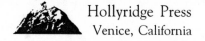

Hollyridge Press
Venice, California

Hollyridge Press
P.O. Box 2872
Venice, California 90294
www.hollyridgepress.com

Cover and Book Design by Rio Smyth
Cover Image by © Sergeybraga | Dreamstime.com
Author photo by P. James Fotos
Manufactured in the United States of America by Lightning Source

ISBN-13: 978-0-9843100-1-2
ISBN-10: 0-9843100-1-0

for Malachi Black
Roger Reese
& Matthew Zapruder

Some of these poems have appeared in:
American Poetry Review, Fence, Forklift,
Opium, Poetry and *Threepenny Review.*

16 15 14 13 12 11 10 09   10 9 8 7 6 5 4 3 2 1

Contents

The Foggist   3

Human Lot   4

You Got a Better Idea?   5

Dear Reader   7

Dear Writer   8

Ode Eventual   9

To Those of You Alive in the Future   10

Pompeii   12

Another Long Day in the Helping Industry   13

Naïf   15

Drunker Etc.   17

Gate Waggled by Wind   18

Off the Hook Ode   19

Loose-Strife   20

My Perspective   21

Thing Is   22

Where I Left Off   23

Scherzo   24

Flyers   25

Bender   26

The Rocket Car   29

Ghost Gust   30

Dream of the Civil Break-Up   31

Hold On   32

Cloud Shadow on Water   33

The Obscurist   34

Quiet Day by the Sea   35

THE FOGGIST

THE FOGGIST

It's important to have no one to talk to.
The people who claimed to know you
were confused or mistaken, their gab
wasted as a diary on what will never happen.
Everything leads away from somewhere.
The startled dove sings its thirteen sorrows
as the fabric of night tightens its stitches
then splits and the miniature mongrels
of the woman who has turned herself blue
with tattoos snivel and roar while
the morning glories declare their immortality
until the sun hits them directly and they shrivel,
insects proclaiming their two deaths, first
that's waking no longer larval, pumping
lymph into new wings, second when the earth
browns and dries and burns and the questions
come to an end. Now that your love has failed,
they want to welcome you back, you who
proceeded so recklessly without a map,
magisterial as a statue crumbling,
who swore night was just a leafing out
of shadows. They have a glass of wine for you,
soup long simmered, the onions alone
have wept for hours. Has it always taken
a winter to form a sentence? How can
even a grape withstand the pressure?
The world's a queasy, disquieted place
where every embrace is pulled apart,
wave-erased in the coming-going business
of the blur that means us neither harm
nor means anything at all.

HUMAN LOT

I'm amazed we haven't crawled off by now.
Later we could go back and cross things out,
that way we wouldn't know where we came from,
the shapes we asked to be bent into.
Sinatra'd be okay again,
mother the same distal approximation,
the sea still trying to spit it out,
and pictures of just any old kittens.
Sometimes your sleep is different than mine.
I can't catch up.
I don't know—there are voices tangled outside.
Wind wants to make me correct something,
the refrigerator says something needs to be pushed
further from the sun.
Out where the sunset ends, they've installed a graveyard
and where it rises, some automatons bash together
mellifluous metal tubing
imparting a festive contusion
to the usual calm disaster of getting out of bed.
To find out why life has this glass sparkle
at the end of a dark hall.
To find out why the paper skeleton holds its hands
demurely over its crotch. Did it fall that way?
To find out how we fell.
There is a name to wake into and music to sleep through.
To find out where the blood comes from on the towels.
Old friends, I believe your betrayals were inadvertent.
To find out if my heart is really unruined.
Father, are you out there
or was your corpse accurate?
Something happened to me when I was young
that I don't want to happen again
but I remember the first smell of ocean,
spark thrust, spark dust,
when the family got out of the car in Jersey
to buy peaches. The road was sand.

YOU GOT A BETTER IDEA?

Why not believe it only took six days
then the almighty, tuckered out, created
another day just to be left alone.
The turtle that holds up the turtle
that holds up the turtle that holds up
the world is held up by another turtle, right?
Eons of random particle motion then
presto! horses and a long battle
in a blizzard so there is no knowing
if any soldier was the last one fighting
then heat-blasted weeds failing to cling
to the impenetrable earth. When Siddhartha
tried of the lubricious wax and honey
of bodies, realizing desire only led
to more desire, he'd still hold a slice
of peach in his lips a few seconds
before chewing and swallowing.
And Jesus on the cross, his tears
turning into bees, looking at his erection
insisting on the monstrous hydraulics
of physical form, tried to distract
his mother by calling to his father
who had appeared to her as nothing too,
not a shower of gold or prize bull
or any other of his literary precursors.
Sometimes it's as if I'm struggling to breathe
on the wrong side of the molecular cascade,
others I'm a stone so porous, one more toss
in the tides and I'm sand.
If they were still on this planet,
I'd have to decide to pity or despise
those two who made me centuries ago
one September night in—I was told—

a boat during a thunder storm
just as I was told death is also nothing.
Why not believe death is also nothing?
Every rose is a wounded mouth.
Why not believe Artaud?
Hello sun with a thorn in your eyes.
I don't think I can help you
but I can sense by the fine bristles
on its antenna how the world is falling apart.
Sometimes I can't believe what passes
for birdsong down here.
All I can say about catching fire
is at first you feel like you can fly
then the soul too comes twisting from the bugle.

DEAR READER

Well, here I am. Or rather, here you are.
I guess I found my own way out. But
weren't we supposed to be tied together?
If not face-to-face, at least you'd have my back.
Sure, some particulars would be nice
in the war between sequitor and non-,
a spike, a spur, a spark among dry cornstalks
but sometimes they just flake away, chaff,
as the days flake to dust and the snow
that fills the breast of every warm-blooded beast
blows away to naught so you'd think
such daily dissolutions wouldn't amount
to much, you forgetting my name, my name
trying to find someone else to attach to.
Who's there? Not that I'm answering.
The sun sinks into its own reflection
although the picture may be upside-down.
Isn't it morning where you are?

DEAR WRITER

Maybe you're the one I've yet to meet
who will take a less myopic part in my bio pic,
who will teach me to throw myself into the wind
like a fiddler, I who have no talent for strings
or woodwinds but have swore allegiance
to what lies cochlea'd inside the tidal shush
inside your own skull. Maybe a less wretched
global positioning comes our way, filibuster
that waylaid both rupture and windfall
ending like a burst vacuum cleaner bag.
Early to dread, early to cry but
I may be your one true abandonment,
accomplice just now being conceived
in your stars. I'm sorry I'm not at liberty
to divulge more, just track backwards
over the same ole song and trance, flattened
like gold into leaf, the impossible
into belief, microcosm of our tenure
on this sympathetic cloud of grief
and yahooing into inebriated dawn.
Just please don't turn around to make sure
I'm keeping up. I'd rather you lose me
than cause delays telling me the way.

ODE EVENTUAL

Only a promise holds the sky to the ground
so I can breath. I lied to everyone I know.
The locusts quiver in expectation of the radio-
promised downpour. Will I ever see you
again? Did I ever? Into the ever-after
shredder goes the never-stops, flying up
startled dove hurtles the procedural
dark. Birthday of fading ink, mother of snow.
The piton holds, keeps its promise to the rope
from which the climber depends, a clause
we depend upon, promise of tomorrow driven
into the granite of today, hope's claw. I'm not
saying we're all not swaying over the drop,
fraying, snap or not, even the word breaks, rock-
face breaks, the at-most of the atmosphere
nothing and nothinger the further you go.
Hour after hour you'll never know.
Sometimes you can stir ash and still remember
ember enough. Sometimes just smoke-smudge,
crushed red flyer, almost a relief
like the priest mispronouncing your pal's
name at the funeral then green rain.

TO THOSE OF YOU ALIVE IN THE FUTURE

who somehow have found a sip of water,
on this day in the past, four syndicated
series involving communication with the dead
were televised and in this way we resembled
our own ghosts in a world made brief with flowers.
To you, our agonies and tizzies
must appear quaint as the stiff shoulders
of someone carrying buckets from a well
or the stung beekeeper gathering honey.
Why did we bother hurrying from A to B
when we'd get no further than D, if that?
On Monday, it sleeted in Pennsylvania
while someone's mother was scoured further
from her own mind. A son-in-law smoked
in the parking lot, exhaling white curses
torn apart by the large invisible.
The general anesthetic wore off
and a woman opened her eyes to the results.
In this way our world was broken and glued.
But why did we bother shooing away the flies?
Did we think we could work our way
inside a diamond if we ground more pigment
into the tooth, tried to hold fire on our tongues,
sucked at the sugars of each other?
Many the engagement rings in the pawnshop.
Many the empties piled at the curbs.
A couple paused on a bridge to watch
chunks of ice tugged by bickering currents.
One who slept late reached out
for one who wasn't there. Breads, heavy
and sweet were pulled from the wide infernos
of stone ovens. My name was Dean Young,

I wrote it on a leaf. Sometimes
we could still manage to get lost,
there were no wires inside most of us yet.
Laughter might come from a window
lit far into the night, others were dark
and always silent.

POMPEII

I can still feel the egg I came from.
I'm fighting my way to the coronation
of a vast vibration. I want fucked
into a sunflower. Don't think for a moment
I have done what I will hate myself for
forever yet. Between the moment fire
is held in the fingers and the next philosophy,
someone puts a tooth on your pillow. Even
when you lose everything, everything won't
let you be lost. Don't roses soar?
You piled racecars at your dying father's feet.
After he died, he kept taking you to the seashore.
Only a simple black line stops
the figure from becoming entirely abstract.
For us, even the sand resists description,
even a dead rabbit. All ash isn't the same.
We enter through zero. You must choose
with great effort to exist, whale
or cricket or headlight. It's safe
to say I speak for no one.

ANOTHER LONG DAY
IN THE HELPING INDUSTRY

I've been grinding my teeth again,
my bike helmet filled with floral goo.
Think of this as a dream if it helps
and I know I try to. Ghost in eddies,
accusatory driftwood, squirrels eating
the birdhouse, the air tolling of roasted
meat. It's stuck 10 o'clock on the draped
statue's visage, the crossing-guard of
emptiness waving me on against the light.
Think of this as happening in a graveyard
if you must, a funny farm I'd rather.
The monster on his ice berg hopes for a remake,
he has a ready jingle, a yen for a peppier
end. The stars are completely pulled apart
but that's not our job. Bats skein
from under the bridge as the planet cranks
into evening. Not our job either.
Unless we increase our gravity,
Daffy Duck will surely tug us into the sky.
Think of Daffy as a parade balloon but
enough about you. I've been at it so long,
I don't know what's preparation and what's
just ordinary maintenance of life.
One must aspire towards weightlessness
to enter the sky yet be resistant
to accentuate the tug, the whole do-not-
go-gentle-into-the-dark stuff. I
do not know which to prefer, the feeling
of letting go or the rope burns
making it, along with a few priors,
impossible for me to accept public office
although I protest the current policy

regarding human composting. Every citizen
should have the right to grow a cherry tree
from his or her chipper-shredded skull.
Little else is known of me save my brief
adult life in various sowing circles
and swimming holes. At times, on summer lawns,
I appeared to be in conversation with fireflies.

NAÏF

Nay, it seems but moments ago
I was flitching mealy apricots
with some other nere-do-wells
in the hung upside-down chicken
of a boundless summer afternoon.
I had hoped to become an interplanetary
meteorologist or leaper of swans
but distractions overwhelmed me
as an orchard is by tent caterpillars.
Such are the pitfalls of a youth
of few cares, a fear of death
that remained abstract, fuzzy and vague,
no more personal than a penny's minting.
I thought for me there was always another
peony, another ant to root for negotiating
hellish terrain, another insane neighbor
loosing her mongrel miniatures. The pink
fade-out of dawn and dusk an instruction
forgot in every hour's loud light
and suffocated dark. Oh bugler,
I don't think you'll ever get it right
but try again. There's always another
beach, waves huge and unorphaned
and collapsed until there's not, another
café although half the time the music's
intolerable, rock-a-billy or French rap.
But mother, this is not way to join
the New York City Ballet, no way
to be a doctor of Martian clouds.
I wrapped myself in tin foil
to be a robot at the party but
kept pulling in Precambrian radio warnings.
I parachuted, needed to feed

on something other than thistle, have sex
not with figments, paint barns for money.
It took all of life and most of dream life
in a morass of details like dandelion fluff
and measles. What used to take a pickup
an afternoon now required expanses
of bubble-wrap, a cavalcade of cardboard,
the unassisted wind no longer able
to carry me off. And now who
is that wrinkled moron in the mirror?
What will assuage his moonstruck gaze?
Do you think he'll buy me a hamster?

DRUNKER ETC.

It's not just a choice between fire or ice,
between Bosch or Botticelli,
the Bright Eternity or the Dark one.
There's the Eternity of Unwritten
Thank You Notes and Waiting on Hold
for someone in India to straighten out
your internet connection.
In front of poetry, a brick wall of prose.
Is it rumor? No, Pavarotti has died.
Finally you realize your teacher's an animal too.
You wait for the elevator down
to the hospital cafeteria wondering
if anything will be different when you get back.
You stable color copies of your cat
with three phones numbers below
to the telephone poles in the neighborhood.
Not even January, already you've shoveled
your driveway seven times. How long
does it take to learn how to fold
an origami rose? For a whole year
you said nothing about how you felt.
Then the tequila goes round the fire
and after a swig you're supposed to admit
what you can't live without.

GATE WAGGLED BY WIND

Those bent pipes in the basement
also hold world together, badged
with rust. Your parents dead, orchard
plowed under, marriage over but that piece of tape
on the wall only seems like it's doing nothing.
Dust too holds world together, fills cracks,
fills the graves so we don't have to watch
beloveds defaced. A comfortable nothingness
takes possession of the heart relinquishing
all claims to what it loves, sweetening
injury, devoted now only to sweeping
three stone steps in the spacious twilight
for the never-to-arrive. What heroism
to care for a cricket. What slow conversation
with the moon. How steady one must be
to keep autumn housed in June. Some part of me
will always be waiting, some part always
gone. Disagreement is in the stars.

OFF THE HOOK ODE

Even if the wine glass can't hold wine,
it looks in one piece. Such satisfaction
when we think we can fix something.

No need to make a long list of fuck-ups
and regrets, it'll look like everyone else's.
It's not like there's a shortage of explanations.

By the fourth day, the roses in the vase
are experts at falling apart but they were
experts even while they were still connected

to the dirt. So were the beetles. Maybe
only details matter: what the flames felt like
before you knew they were flames, bits

of the porous world, the words that made up
your intimate code. How have we gotten so snarled?
Sometimes thunder promises rain but it's wrong

and birds fly the wrong direction so why
should you worry you're turning to frost
in summer? Even the wind contradicts itself

and the one who thinks he has the most to say
is the one doing most of the not-talking
which isn't necessarily listening while

the other goes on in half-asleep defiance
so he gets the gist just as brushing fingertips
on a monument conveys great bulk and weight

but look at it: the angel seems just alighted
to scourge twilight from the mind, let the body
fill with stone. Nothing can be fixed.

LOOSE-STRIFE

Everyone feels they got here from very far away,
not just the astronauts and divorcees and poets.
Some want to lose the directions how to get back,
for others it's a long time without cell phone reception.
Nothing here can be drawn with a ruler,
not even rain although even this high up
there are beer trucks. What feels like a hook
pulled from deep inside may be an old wisteria vine.
Give it ten years. When twilight comes
from the lake in the lake's blue mask,
you might think you'll never have to pretend again,
from now on you'll know yourself
but that's only because that self is disappearing.
You're right, when your mother died,
she *did* turn into a peregrine. I don't know how
I can be so cruel to those who love me
or how they can be to me. Sometimes a rock
comes hurtling down the path
but there's no one above you.

MY PERSPECTIVE

An unlimited fruit-cup would be nice.
And briefer liaisons with the destructive
dryads who always tag along. Flying's not
the problem it once was now that everyone's
turned out to be a constellation. So much
for today's wish-list. Now for the narrative.
Sorry, there isn't one although time passing
makes it feel like we've moving squarely forward
to a point where everything comes together
to be sorted out, what you overheard
in the cloak room that hurt you, the description
of the herding habits of bats, a nun
you once knew who ceased to be a nun
and lived out her days selling lurid paintings
of waves, all the lost thinking about the new.
Somewhere out there it all meets up
and vanishes, undistracted, dictating
a law that makes things volumetric and solid
and shrink, in proportion just as long as you don't
shake your head. It's not brain surgery.
But what is? Can smells work? They get in there,
don't they? Can dreams be controlled by wires?
Isn't beauty a mistake? Wouldn't it be better
to blend in but into what? Something sticky,
I'll wager, then bleached. But who's to say
these errant arcs of thought, chopped-up
vignettes, feckless sit-com confessions
in rooms under water, in July, in blue snow
don't forecast our role in the grand epic?
It sure doesn't feel harmless.
It feels like being thrown.

THING IS

People I have not seen for a long time
will recognize me instantly.
What kind of transformation is that?
What kind of life-threatening syndrome?
How many erasures have I rubbed apart
to still be this same smudge?
Someone else has already written this poem
so I'm gonna relax.
The whole mousetrap in the darkness of life thing.
The beautiful circles wrecked to compose all things thing.
The rust-proofing the under-carriage ruse.
After a while you have to stop listening
to people telling you you need more insurance.
You live across the street from the fire-station,
even that sort of excitement dies out.
You can sleep through anything
and the whole never waking up thing.
The meadow turned yellow by eternal longing.
Who believes in that sort of shit?
Me apparently.
Apparently that was me writing on the blackboard
the Keats quote about rioting in luxurious imagination.
With enough nitrous oxide I can leave my cavitied body in the chair
and cross to the stationary store
and buy sticker roses from the one-armed cashier.
If magnesium sulfate is brought into contact with a molybium substrate
a most wondrous glow is produced.
Myriad the throttling of sunlight upon this earth.
Which too glows.
Which too is made of glass,
winged beings diaphanous above the summer corpse.
My darlings, all my darlings, is there a song
you have yet to shatter me with?
Golden is the shutter of the sea.
These chains too conspire our salvation.

WHERE I LEFT OFF

I've been here my whole life still I'm somewhere else.
The whole plummeting through space thing.
The song that can't be listened to without pathos become bathos.
The whole is it the other way around? thing.
Someone is claiming he's invented a new fist.
The trampoline's been around a long time
but we're still held down, held back.
Can history be changed by blinking fast?
There are people who do absolutely nothing all day.
I'd hate to hamper their equipoise or depression, whatever.
Dominic though, that little twit, I'm ready to twist apart.
The believers in idiot babble of children talking to paper dolls.
But one of the golden moments was when I went to April's studio
and she was welding copper star after star,
I pretended to descript for a magazine
when I just wanted to fuck her
right there among the fat dashed-down sparks
holding onto their hot thoughts.
What did I care what do I care what will I care?
No one has to rehearse to be a child
but it takes practice to disintegrate.
Is my intention the abandonment of intention?
Is that how we get absolved and become pollen or talc
instead of gargoyles in a sea of dwarfs?
I hope they leave me in the road
to be run over another hundred times
so even my hips open like wings.

SCHERZO

The tree meditates as it burns.
You are singing you just don't know it

yet. Who is the angel with his foot
on the dragon's neck? Who is the dragon?
We are moved by the polarities of grass.
Kafka tries to wish us well,
Tolstoy tries to wish us well

but they have no idea the empire
we're dealing with. The spill-overs
clot, its geysers rot into a million Bibles,
its ash is ash. We have spent not nearly

enough time asleep together.
I don't think the soul goes anywhere.
Or away. Hello darkling, I'm sorry.

Myriad the disconnection holding world together.
Myriad my love for you shatters.

I sat half the afternoon on suspicious carpet
teaching the little wiry dog my name
least I go unrecognized in paradise.

FLYERS

I'm trying to figure out how to be absolutely faithful
to something I can't get near.
I guess whatever part of me wasn't born a pile of ash
and didn't get caught in barbed wire was.
But it's easier holding a match
until it snuffs out against your fingers.
Me and my brother used to do that
staring into each other's eyes
while everyone else was having a childhood.
You know how you flinch you lose
and then the angel goes off to whisper
what she'd like done to her in the backseat
into someone else's ear.
I ain't about to let my education go wasted.
I went to this house once with drugs
and they had an honest-to-god tiger on the couch.
It's okay, they said, she's not a year old.
I went from one life to another
stroking that electric fur,
not long but long enough
to see my hand gone through an inferno
and still be my hand.
These were circus people, trapezists
baby-tiger-sitting. I belonged
out on the road somewhere blowing around.
I didn't want to but I did.
The girl, put together like a remote-control glider,
kissed me goodbye on each cheek
like I was getting on the Titanic.
You won't find my real name anywhere.

BENDER

Ever since I lost consciousness,
I keep finding it in the oddest places:
at the barn after the dancers turned to chaff,
in bits of chintz, corn husk, phosphemes of dream
that bob up like newts talking a drink of air.
It's okay, there's nothing so adored
as what's lost, more interrogated
than what's found, the silver sliver
plucked out, melted down for the ongoing ingot
of a life's history as counterweight
to days just whirrs and spin-outs,
hiccups and coughs into bleached handkerchiefs.
I mean something thorny to knock your head against
like a banana tree although I've never seen one,
might be a bush for all I know.
A little knowing goes a long way
but not-knowing reaches universe's end,
scylla'ed by nebulas, chrybdised by black holes.
The world is trivial, is trivia.
In these windows snow is always falling.
Caphaleonomancy is divination
by roasted donkey head. A black bear
may be brown, a brown black. One scavanges,
one kills which makes all the diff
if you run or lie flat. Imagine a fruit
you've never tasted, is it poisonous,
to be peeled or just bit? Each kiss
is further predicament, the star-shaped seeds
drop into your palm, the ta-dum of a child's drum
arterial with the under-girding of some song
unheard like rebar for unpoured concrete,
like a series of likenesses that will vanish
into like into like like the divisions between

those squares of sod laid down upon
this scorched earth so lay thee down, my darling
...and here the station changes itself
as we round the jagged edge of coastal fog,
local dialects of rain that drench and evaporate
like thoughts that can't last in the brain
without words. What bird was it never came back?
A crow? Must we now live without that part
of our shadow? I guess we will be warbled
elsewhere. Somehow we keep departing,
stretching the taffy of the void, losing
each other, coming ashore naked of all
but our wits. Some days I miss the swamps
out back of the old home, UFO sightings
in the heyday of carpal tunnel syndrome,
the apparatchiks in the frescoed luncheonette
dissecting the offhand slips of upper echelon,
my mother knowing who I was or someone like me,
a tally kept naively, Santa Claus imminent.
We all went to separate islands like students
of a correspondence course. No one wanted an orange
as rhyming material thus the moon grew wan
from overuse. A spiral spirituality
rippled the duck pond until absinthe
was decriminalized and everyone went Rimbaud.
Anachronistically, we were brought up short
to the present in dog carts, troikas, cabriolet's,
age-spotted, waylaid by phantom pains,
mishaps with Crazy Glue, one with a pig valve,
one with a tuck or two, a few self-committed.
Still we knew the alarms of the financial gurus
would not endure. Only glint endures, only bling.
And the contact lens prescription will not endure,
only the blur, the angelic, wanton blur,
the oracle's preferred weather, overcast,
prognostication of muddles for meatheads,
scribbled hearts hermetically sealed,

a baby snake settling in the hand,
accepting its warmth as I would yours
if I ever see you again, if I ever saw you once,
surely a good sign like home-sickness
even though we know home no longer exists
nor what soared to its horizon, peregrine
that was not father come back. Come back!
Come back! but nothing does, not the star
in the center of the chest, not the river
of bees that was our honeyed bequest, not
the blizzard that was once the mind. You
were gone before you arrived, say the waves
on the self-erasing beach.

THE ROCKET CAR

—after Kenneth Koch

The rocket car is waiting,
there's someplace specific to go in outer space,
the god particles getting further and further apart
so the mileage goes ways up,
your teacher suddenly taken to the hospital
a long time ago or seconds or not at all
depending on your pressure on the throttle.
Maybe all the tar's coming out of you.
On the window's a decal warning
beyond the speed you're approaching
the body becomes pure electricity
which is okay, it feels familiar
like sorting through those staticy memories
of dying each time you wake
and have forgotten all over again
the rules of compliance.

GHOST GUST

How can a man start out luminous
and end up a smudge? How can you see a river
in the mirror then wipe away the steam
and there's a rock? The voice in the head
sways congress but comes out breach,
a Monday morning falls on Friday eve
like a comet made of darkness. I am
a tree, the ember keeps telling itself
so maybe you don't have to listen
to what the fire says even if you build it,
gather the sticks after the windstorm,
crumble up the sports section, feed it yourself.
But why's my mind a celestial chariot
waking then a worm under corn husk
by afternoon? Maybe by night, woven
in a silk denial of itself, it'll morph
into a winged, already half-dust thing
and rise to some new oblivion or,
singed, fall for frogs to finish off.
So little light gets through even though
there's almost nothing to me
but what a relief, the kind a ghost
must feel after the initial shock
of sparks flying through without a sting,
walking into walls without feeling a thing,
then the cold resignation of never
being touched again.

DREAM OF THE CIVIL BREAK-UP

It's good to get the withering season
over with, throw off the whining and losing
campaign buttons both and come to a blasted
plain where the storms can be seen far off
trying to undress like drunks trying to fuck.
They too are full of trepidation
and fumbled-away anger that they let
things gets so far out of hand or so far
in hand, twisting an arm behind the back
scattering the bouquet of gladiolas
and hatchets, the square peg jammed
into the oh'ing mouth then each getting
goodbyes in early, before the glut
bottoms-out the value. Even if
my rocket ship's a delusional
form of escape, it's still escape.
On to the Mushroom Planet with my cat,
Presto Joe as co-pilot and lots of cans
of lima beans! The earth with its troubles
becomes a swirlly marble. Don't know
how long I can go on like this, not very's
probably the point else all's meaningless,
the heaving ta-ta's, weepy waltz, exchange
of keepsakes on the dock, for you a cinderblock
wrapped in foil symbolizing my heart,
for me a vial of your breath to crush
for one after my last.

HOLD ON

The ant grips low in the breeze.
Like the morning glory, it knows
this is our last day on earth
but that's okay, so was yesterday.
And tomorrow? Ask the mulberry
mangling in the stretched wire fence.
Ask the weather. By evening, we don't know
which fear will triumph, of being alone
or loved. It's complicated, says the bee,
I can't make it any clearer than this dance.
The last months the mother knows no one,
her body becoming hollow as a wren's.
His last, the father sounds caught
in a net. We can ask him anything
and he'll answer, taking a long time
forming the words with a tongue turned to clay
but we don't. Was it jubilation
that made him buy the three-piece yellow suit
he'd wear just twice? Every three steps
he was out of breath, another floating
leaf avoiding the grate as long as possible.
Now things are going wrong inside us:
heart, stomach, throat. We sleep
better in a chair, entertained
by additions to the seven thousand
hours of music we'll never hear again
and cicadas whirring from shells
of smaller selves the cat loves
to chase and crush.

CLOUD SHADOW ON WATER

Let the bells drown, let the rain down.
Don't love the bougainvillea ever again,
it's vibrant profusion's a net of thrones.
Don't love the wine anymore, its mineral tints

and autumn breeze coming through an open door
ruffling pages of a book not worth finishing.
Don't love the Kandinsky print
that once seemed a parade of jubilant,

geometric souls or the neighbor's sad-eyed
dog who'd hold your hand loosely in her jaws
and ask nothing else. To be asked nothing else
is to be asked too much. Not one more

volt of touch, not another wet glance above
the wobbling candles. No more opera
or freak folk, enough of Monk's ruby lurch
into elegance, enough of deer leaping

ahead of the car on the ridge, no more
owls or howling in the wood, enough of these stars.
It's possible to grow sick even of forgiveness
so please don't tell me you'll understand

if I let you. Rather the letter never
sent, never written, rather let the bells
down, the hours hollow. It's cool here
by the water as dark comes on, twisting

beneath the surface invisible forms
while bats zig and jag, snagging the smallest
denizens of the air. Sweetheart, already
I'm almost not anywhere.

THE OBSCURIST

You can't grab blossoms.
You can only grab god. You can't
grab god, you can only be devoured
by the waterfall, spit out by snakes—
a busy afternoon. Don't forget
the monarch-winged skeleton
hung from the chandelier
as part of your instruction. A chandelier
not made of ice is a waste of liquidation.
Death is a waste of liquidation.
Do you think the miraculous is only
what you've never seen? The dog
sleeps on the couch, you see that, right?
She's about to take off her costume.
And how about when tears illuminate
even the nothing lit? I can't help you
anymore than you can help me.
No single point will assert its vanishing,
the mantis tall as the flagship,
the pricked finger a nova.
Ergo, hold this broken bolt against your chest
until it shares your fever, evening star.
Let's get you out of these wet things.
With enough practice we may become
an orchard. I was given a mechanical
rabbit as part of my instruction.
The dog turns gray as a formality.
The vines proliferate as a formality.
Something inside us always counts backwards.
We exit through zero. Even in rapids,
we find our rest.

QUIET DAY BY THE SEA

This life doesn't fit you,
not long enough, tight across the chest,
vexingly concaved
but it's like that for everyone
accounting for the constant rattle
even in the mountains where you'd expect
silence would drown everything out,
all that squawk and backroar.
A dollop of purposefulness might be nice,
to be guided as an octopus is through the inky night
but no such luck.
The inner glitter of what we once were—
dryads of twisted silver wire?
A nearly vicious vigor in every hour
was okay while it lasted,
it got stuff done, sequestered and hammered off.
But it's okay now too,
a nap stolen from the waves of afternoon,
the droll wonder that one's legs
still work, starlight drizzle,
an answer from beyond the attic.

LaVergne, TN USA
28 December 2009
168204LV00003B/320/P